The Classical Tradition in Modern Art

The Classical

Other Books by Walter Pach

Ananias or the False Artist

Vincent Van Gogh

Georges Seurat

Masters of Modern Art

Ingres

The Art Museum in America

Tradition in Modern Art

by WALTER PACH

New York • Thomas Yoseloff, *Publishers* • London

© 1959 by Sagamore Press, Inc.

Library of Congress Catalogue Card Number: 59-7853

Thomas Yoseloff, *Publisher*
11 East 36th Street
New York 16, N. Y.

Thomas Yoseloff Ltd.
123 New Bond Street
London W. 1, England

Printed in the United States of America

TO
NIKIFORA

whose feeling for the classics of her native Greece has made her the most sympathetic of listeners as I read her these pages on the later classics.

Contents

Introduction   13

The Classicism of Delacroix   20

The Classicism of Barye   29

Some Notes on Delacroix   33

The Later Masters   37

Plates

1. Greek, fifth century, B.C.   The Ilyssus from the Parthenon
2. Géricault   Leda
3. Jean Goujon   The Rivers of France
4. Poussin   The Realm of Flora
5. Watteau   The Judgment of Paris
6. Louis David   The Sabines (detail)
7. Delacroix   Fresco at Valmont
8. Delacroix   Autumn
9. Delacroix   The Sibyl with the Golden Bough
10. Pompeiian Art   Woman with a Shield
11. Pompeiian Art   Man and Woman
12. Delacroix   Heliodorus
13. Raphael   Heliodorus
14. Pompeiian Art   Centauress and Bacchante
15. Delacroix   Centauress and Bacchante
16. Delacroix   Achilles and the Centaur
17. Barye   Nude
18. Greek, about 400 B.C.   Girl with Cap
19. Barye   Lapith (Theseus) and Centaur
20. Barye   Three Graces
21. Barye   Jaguar and Hare

22. Barye   Leopard Resting
23. Ingres   The Bather of Valpinçon
24. Ingres   Mme. Ingres
25. Corot   Hagar and Ishmael
26. Corot   Woman with a Pearl
27. Leonardo da Vinci   Mona Lisa
28. Baron Gros   Self Portrait
29. Pompeiian Art   The Baker and His Wife
30. Courbet   Woman with a Parrot
31. Manet   Bar at the Folies Bergères
32. Renoir   Mother and Child
33. Renoir   Girls Bathing
34. Renoir   Two Women with Flowered Hats
35. Cézanne   The Clockmaker
36. Cézanne   Landscape
37. Cézanne   Still Life
38. Cézanne   Water Color
39. Seurat   The Clearing
40. Seurat   Boys Bathing
41. Seurat   The Circus
42. Matisse   Mme. Matisse
43. Matisse   Odalisque with Magnolias
44. Picasso   Female Nude
45. Picasso   Nymph
46. Duchamp-Villon   Torso of a Young Man
47. Greek, fifth century B.C.   Warrior of Aegina
48. Duchamp-Villon   Baudelaire
49. French, thirteenth century   Head
50. Derain   Head

The Classical Tradition in Modern Art

1

Introduction

IT IS WITH GREAT CONFIDENCE THAT I APPROACH THE WRITING OF THIS book. Why should I not feel so when the subject, classical art in our time, is so inspiring? I shall have to produce a perfect masterpiece of bad writing if I am to obscure the optimism one must feel over the prospects ahead of us. Indeed, our pleasure in the art to come must be in proportion to the gloom felt by too many people over conditions today. The atom bomb is terrifying enough, to be sure, and for ill-prepared interpreters of the idea that art reveals future conditions, the present state of affairs would mean impending annihilation: we look in vain for anyone to say that the new generation of painters can show us valid replacement of the great men who have been dying off so rapidly in recent years. Where is there today a Matisse, a Bonnard, a Derain, a Rouault, a Dufy, or a Juan Gris? Even such exciting arts as theirs are diminished, moreover, when we think of their immediate predecessors, Cézanne, Renoir, and Seurat.

13

If we take comfort for a moment in Picasso, Braque, and Villon, we can scarcely avoid seeing future chaos when they finally leave us. and when we have nothing but the welter of inferior talents or non-talents that now fill public and private galleries. And so Hamlet's words are in the mouths of many artists today: "The time is out of joint. O cursed spite: that ever I was born to set it right!" But the very fact that this pessimism had reached the stage of being a proverb is proof of the fact that men have felt in the same way, times without number, before. And yet the end of the world has obstinately declined to appear—not even when a Michelangelo spoke in such a strain of disillusion. His sure vision that the glories of the Renaissance were subsiding, as the men he called "great fools" misapplied his effort, is well remembered, and it ought to be a warning against seeing the present decadence as final. Before Michelangelo the prophets of gloom, backed by religion, had far more right to see destruction ahead when the great Christian art of the Middle Ages was going down before the onslaught of returning paganism.

And by the same token, what must have been the dismay of the Greeks when they saw darkness following the unequaled light they had given the world. Its first enemy was the brute force of the Romans, those "verbose pillagers," as Renoir called them; afterward came ascetic Christianity and the Orientalism of the Byzantines. No, the evil thoughts which haunt the world's mind today have a far smaller right to their hold on us than the despair which has faced civilization again and again in the past.

I believe that the art museum, rightly approached, can show us every reason for faith in those human resources which have triumphed so often—and in the teeth of greater odds against us. At another time of crisis, one near enough for us to appreciate the terror which filled men's minds over the "deluge" which Louis XV saw as the successor of his adorable eighteenth century, Voltaire jeered at the complacent belief in the past which made of all change a menace; he proved that if the earlier centuries could show supreme achievements, the modern time, his time, had its own sufficient word to say about various great matters overlooked by the pessimists; thus the balance of merit never sank decisively from a supposed golden age, gone beyond recovery.

I return to Renoir and quote again a couple of sentences he spoke.

The idea they carry with them—of a constant and legitimate renewal of hope—is surely apposite, above all with the explanation of it in his opening words: "There is nothing outside the classics. To please a student, even the most princely, a musician could not add another note to the seven of the scale. He must always come back to the first one again, an octave higher or lower. Well, in art it is the same thing. But one must see that the classic may appear at any period. Poussin was a classic; Père Corot was a classic. When I was a student, Corot was unknown, Delacroix and Ingres were laughed at; the men considered great were Scheffer and Delaroche. That seems strange today, but it was really so."

It is so strange indeed that, to believe it, we need all the authority of one who witnessed the state of affairs a hundred years ago. Renoir goes on to say what brought about these conditions, and we see that the same cause is producing the same effect—ignorance supported by alleged authority was the reason why a Delaroche (now utterly discredited) was preferred to a Delacroix. But have we gone far enough? Do we see that an error of almost greater importance was committed— and is still being committed—by the majority of people? They are guilty of such an error when they give to Ingres alone the merit of representing the classics, and think of Delacroix, despite his protests, as a "mere romantic." His writings bristle with material showing how well founded was his claim to be, as he said, "a pure classicist," and it will be one of the purposes of this book to give material evidence in support of that claim.

For over thirty years I have been convinced that the essentials of his art derived from the purest of classical sources and, beginning in 1930, I published articles in Paris defending this idea. Three of them, which have never before been printed in English, are included in the present volume. One article is mainly devoted to Barye, Delacroix's friend and, in sculpture, the exact upholder of the conception that his contemporary expressed through painting (and through words). At times, after the years separating the three articles, especially the third one (twenty years after the second), I repeated previously stated ideas so that the reader might know what had gone before. It would be easy to iron out these repetitions, but I prefer to think that the present public will be indulgent of them in the interest of greater clarity.

And now, having always admired the lawyer's advice—"Define your terms"—I think I am due for a brief explanation of what my oft-recurring words, classical and romantic, mean or ought to mean, for they have been all too loosely used—by innumerable people. In one of my Paris articles I spoke of the almost grotesque error of speaking of the movie actor's classical nose or curls. As if the genius that found its apotheosis in Greece were concerned with such externals, instead of being—and uniquely—a matter of the spirit! Again, one may accept such a statement as "Rembrandt is the great classic of the Dutch School," only if one has in mind the fact that, essentially, he is not classical, but romantic.

When we come down to definitions we find ourselves in pretty complete accord as to the classical qualities. They have been described again and again as expressions (most frequently Greek) of our need for unity and variety, balance, proportion, and so on. Such qualities may appear in any period and be a result of man's quest for perfection in forms not necessarily traceable to the Greeks, though in the centuries since the time of that people, Greek influence has been so strong that it may be seen in arts long considered to be the reverse of the classical. Thus the word Gothic, adopted as a term of contempt for medieval work supposed to be in revolt against antiquity, applies to the cathedral of Reims where many figures are obviously derived from statuary of Greco-Roman origin. Found in the vicinity, the ancient works were joyfully followed by the Gothic carvers who adorned the great building, even if its soaring lines—a romantic gesture if there ever was one—contrasted so flagrantly with the static character of the Greek temple.

Misunderstanding of the romantic has been far more widespread and injurious than what we have just observed as regards the classic. Perhaps the word romantic is itself at fault, suggesting, as it does, ruined castles in the moonlight, or the love affairs of the young, or their dreams of glory in distant lands. But again, these are only superficial aspects of the matter, like the classical brow, and as such the victim of at least a covert derision.

But the romantic is a necessary complement to the classic; it is quite as much a force in human affairs, and as fully entitled to our admiration. The classical tends to the loss of movement, for its perfection acts as a brake on our effort to reach new values—and today (perhaps of all days) the vista of our possibilities seems more boundless than ever before. We grasp in only the vaguest way what the scientific discoveries of the last hundred and fifty years have done in changing man's conception of the world and of life. As for what lies immediately before us in the peaceful utilization of the atom for instance, it may well be that the wildest prophets of the new age are falling short of the realities to come about. The advent of museums, giving us a vastly extended understanding of the past, is even more notable when we consider what we have derived from arts like the Asian, the Mexican, the African, the Polynesian, and others. It is long since that they discredited the idea of the artist as one who simply "holds the mirror up to nature"; only the most simple minded still believe in that misinterpretation of Shakespeare (who warned us against it with his interjected phrase "as t'were").

Now all this change in our basic principles is part of our debt to the element of romanticism. Renoir, immediately following his phrase "there is nothing outside of the classics," goes on to tell of their differences of aspect when creative men like Poussin and Corot do their work, romantic work, as Delacroix confirms for us when he speaks his audacious word as to a chief classic of French literature: "Racine was a romantic for the people of his time, for all time he is classical, which is to say perfect." You will find the words again in one of my Paris articles, but I make no apology for giving a second mention in this book to an idea of such capital importance.

Consider how romantic is the quality of originality. In all periods it has been recognized as something necessary for really great art: Michelangelo made one of his bitterest thrusts at Raphael when he said that the younger man's work showed more of study than of talent. Classical perfection, what Raphael's followers admire in him most of all, is the goal of the studious man—an artist like Michelangelo is a breaker of new ground. In his youth he had proved that he could successfully compete with the past; in his maturity his romantic faculty makes him original, creative.

If, then, my present purpose is that of showing the basically classic qualities in Delacroix and Barye, I believe I have now cleared myself of any lack of admiration for the romantic principle. Not only was it the phase of their work which most impressed the public, but it was for a long time what united them with their successors. For over a hundred years the first thing we notice about these later men is that they are of the creative type and therefore again romantics. Pure classicism implies no interest in the ever more rapidly changing forms of the moderns—you can be as perfect in one form as another. And yet, as I hope to show in the last section of this book, each one of the great nineteenth- or twentieth-century artists to be discussed has his share in the classical virtues.

Indeed, when we come to Picasso, the central figure in the modern movement, we shall see that cubism, which contains his chief contribution to the art of our time, is essentially classical. Abandoning as it does all the romantic appeal of the visible world, it concentrates on such problems as balance, movement, and space. In the masterpiece here reproduced from Picasso's cubistic period (see Plate 44) it is qualities of impersonal rightness that he seeks—and finds. For those who do not yet see this to be the truth, I offer another example of the man's work, that lithograph of the recumbent figure which, inescapably, is of the type of beauty celebrated by John Keats in his *Ode to a Grecian Urn* (see Plate 45).

Can any real understanding of the *Ilyssus from the Parthenon,* let us say, permit us to think that classical art died or was lost when the Greeks lapsed into silence? Géricault gives a first answer to any such heresy (see Plates 1 and 2). The chance resemblance of the two torsos makes it easier for us to see their essential likeness—it is in the fact that both the ancient and the modern genius can take something straight out of nature and invest it with art of the highest quality. The nobility of Géricault's drawing tells us that "the glory that was Greece" still has its survivals today.

Roman art is more than doubtful as a continuator of the Greek— every new visit to the museum puts us more on our guard against Roman imitations of the Greeks. And as for the Renaissance, we have practically given up the idea that it is a rebirth of antiquity—it is a rebirth of human genius. The marvelous things in a Donatello or a Leonardo spring from man's need for the classical virtues and not from his new and romantic contact with antiquity. The understanding of that period was still quite limited during the lifetime of those two masters, and so Benvenuto Cellini could safely boast that when he restored the missing parts of an ancient sculpture, no one could tell where the original ended and where his own work began. With our present-day knowledge of the difference between the two periods of art, I have seen the veriest laymen in Florence distinguish accurately between Cellini's handiwork and the ancient part of the sculpture, thus proving that the Renaissance differed fundamentally from the period of Greece and Rome.

The open secret of the whole matter is, therefore, that the classical qualities are not things of a period but eternal. The same applies to the romantic qualities. They are to be seen already in pre-historic art. Our first impression from it is that of the extraordinary observation of animals and the uncanny skill of the men who delineated them. But then come thoughts of the purpose of these artists. It was not to display their mastery of drawing, though of late paleologists have been talking of schools for drawing in the very ancient time. No, the great urge to the men of Altamira, Lascaux, and the other centers was expression, the romantic impulse.

And so, from the beginning, the two sources of art, the classical and the romantic, have continued side by side. It is probable that the rendering of new ideas, the romantic element, gets the first response—of admiration or opposition—from the public. Hence the vigor with which Delacroix and Barye, for example, were attacked, and defended. Baudelaire, in his magnificent poem, *Les Phares,* places Delacroix with Michelangelo and Rembrandt, and we shall see with what supreme men Gautier and Silvestre compare Barye. The opponents of the two great artists were equally unhesitating in their use of strong terms of disparagement. All of which speaks of the romantic fervor of the period. I have tried to show in the articles which follow that, underlying the battle of the nineteenth century, was the solid basis of the classics.

2

The Classicism of Delacroix

WHEN ONE CARES DEEPLY FOR AN ART, ONE IS ASTONISHED TO LEARN that there are intelligent people who do not like it. When one cares for Delacroix, one seizes every chance to see his painting and one infallibly comes to place it among the highest conquests of European genius. But then, when talking to men whose culture is not absolutely negligible, one perceives that they have looked—occasionally—at works by the master, and that they recognize in them little more than amplitude of composition. They consider even that quality as not exempt from a certain theatrical tinge, they see imperfections, and indeed a swollen look to the drawing. Summing up, they admit that he is an artist of great "historical" importance, whose school, that of romanticism, produced works that are remarkable, to be sure, but that the public may quite properly neglect at times in order to concentrate on things more modern, more unknown—or more permanent.

Tiresome as it is to spend time, even a moment of time on such

erroneous opinions, the fact that they represent the idea of Delacroix
held by no less than a majority of collectors, museum men, and artists
is a sufficient excuse for having mentioned the matter. The idea most
contrary to theirs, the one to be demonstrated here—as criticism ought
to have done long ago—is that the essential quality of Delacroix is his
classicism. And it is the more remarkable because it derives from his
inmost nature, permitting him therefore to move about with ease in an
art which his eyes have never seen—the painting of the Greeks, as represented by works of the decadence at Pompeii and Rome; they still give
us our idea of antique painting.

Before indicating the reasons for defending a thesis as to Delacroix
so little accepted and so difficult to support by material proofs, let us
see what written testimony reveals the classical side of the master's
mind. We know from two articles which appeared in the *Gazette des
Beaux-Arts* for 1927, how solid was the foundation which Delacroix's
years at the Lycée Impérial gave him in the matter of the Greek and
Latin writers. He never lost contact with them and, very late in life,
declared that it is a public shame for the government to support schools
which do not require from their pupils an acquaintance with the
ancient authors. We are reminded of Cézanne's reflection on his own
early years: "There was good study of the humanities at that time."

Yet it is in our artist's remarks on the share of the classic in painting that we must seek the written explanations of the idea we are in-
sisting on; and the reader of Delacroix's *Journal*, of his *Literary Works*
or his *Letters* knows that, in the matter of quotations, there is only an
embarrassment of choice. The student of his writing knows that the
intellect of the painter made him pursue his investigation of the nature
of beauty along the lines of literature and music as well as along those
of his own art. A single example must suffice here. In 1857, when about
to enter his sixties, he wrote on "The Antique" in his *Notes for a Dic-
tionary of the Fine Arts:*

Whence comes that special quality, that perfect taste which exists only
in the antique? Perhaps from our comparing with it all the things people
have done in their attempt to imitate it. But what can one possibly compare with what has been done to perfection, and along the most diverse
lines of effort? I do not see what is lacking in Virgil, in Horace. I see clearly
what I should like to find in our greatest writers, and also what I should

wish to see removed from them. . . . But it is above all in what remains to us of the plastic arts of the ancients that that quality of taste and of perfect measure is found at the highest point. We can withstand a comparison with them in literature; in the arts—never.

Titian is one of those who approach the spirit of the antique most closely. He is of the family of the Dutchmen and consequently of the antique. He knows how to work from nature: that is what always makes one feel a genuineness of type in his pictures; therefore it is no fugitive type, the kind of thing that derives from imagination in a man who, having imitators, soon disgusts us with them. One might say that there is a grain of madness in all the others; he alone spells good sense, being master of himself, of his facility and his execution: it never dominates him, and he never parades it. We think to imitate the antique when we transcribe it word for word, so to speak, when we caricature its draperies, etc. Titian and the Flemish have the spirit of the antique and not the imitation of its external forms.

A few pages before, he had written:

Rubens is more heroic than certain antiques. He had a similar genius. It is the mind that is everything. Ingres has nothing Homeric about him except his pretentions. He makes tracings of the exterior. Rubens is a Homer through painting the spirit and neglecting mere outer dress, or rather in painting the dress of his own period.

In the grandiose audacity of such lines, one sees clearly the concept of the classic in Delacroix. It is entirely within the realm of principles, and contains nothing of that superficial use of the word which we get from a man who thinks he sees Greek style in a given building because it has a façade with a pediment and columns, or who would speak of a nose or a drapery as classic because of a resemblance with models borrowed from the antique. Delacroix condemns any such idea in his essay on Poussin:

That is the art of the antiquary, not of the artist—who must rise to the level of the spirit, to the sense of what he appropriates while imitating it. Man is the subject of his study, by way of the antique. . . . Such is Poussin's imitation. That of the moderns, on the contrary, that which prevails in painting and in architecture, is completely given over to minutiae. Little details, placed with a research that is more pedantic than exact, believe themselves to be resurrections of the antique.

No, the man who wrote those astonishing words "of the family of the Dutchmen and *consequently* of the antique," understood that classicism resides in that current of thought which aims at harmony through the proportions, through unity, through equilibrium. It is that last term which makes us think of the complementary (and not opposed) current of our minds, which is romanticism. An equilibrium having been established, the oscillation of the scales having ceased, we arrive at an absence of movement contrary to that human need which makes us break a balance in order to find another balance, which makes us pierce the known horizon in order to push on beyond it toward a new horizon that no one had suspected before.

Delacroix, although distrustful of the ill-founded and negative romanticism of a great number of his contemporaries, never dreamed of denying the contribution of his school to the mind of his period. On the contrary, in those same passages of the *Journal* of 1857, he defines the tendency that people attribute to him—and with justice—through the most striking example in French literature. "Racine was a romantic for the people of his time. For all time he is classical, which is to say perfect. Respect for tradition is nothing else than observing the laws of taste, without which no tradition can be durable."

In another place he wrote: "One cannot sufficiently repeat that the rules for Beauty are eternal, changeless, and the forms of Beauty are variable. What decides on these rules, with their ever different externals? Taste alone, as rare perhaps as beauty: that taste which causes us to discern beauty whenever it appears, and which makes us recognize it in the great artists who have the gift of inventing."

Having been in the front line of those artists who have the gift of inventing, his own taste makes him "discern" (in the most exact sense of the word) the beauty of an art which he knew only by feeble echoes, but the memory of which had been deposited within him by the memory of the human race as it reached back to antiquity and recalled the masterpieces of that period. It is in this way, I believe, that we are obliged to explain the relationship of Delacroix's painting with that of the Greeks. At once, when one has got the idea of such a relationship, the proofs of its profound influence on the modern painter begin their constant accumulation, and it is perhaps because of the rarity of ancient paintings that we have been so long about realizing that Delacroix is their greatest inheritor.

At the Metropolitan Museum in New York, there have been exhibited since 1903 a series of frescoes of the highest importance. They come from Boscoreale, a villa discovered near Herculaneum. It was these paintings, of which one is reproduced in this volume (see Plate 10), which first suggested to me the aesthetic kinship of Delacroix with that school, still a Greek school, even if represented by provincial artists, and of the decadence. In a book on modern art I had affirmed a fact for which I had sometimes received confirmation when accompanying competent visitors to the Pompeiian room which they were seeing for the first time. It sufficed to draw their attention to the "modern" cross-hatching on the shield of the feminine personage shown in our reproduction and to ask what artist of our period might have executed this passage in the work—at once the answer came, "Why, Delacroix!" The astonishment which always accompanied the observation proved that criticism had neglected this essential phase of the master's genius. In the whole of his immense work, the detail most exactly fitted to put us on the right track had remained all but unnoticed. I refer to three experiments in fresco hidden away at Valmont, in Normandy, in the property of a cousin of Delacroix's, and unknown to the majority of students of his work. In 1834, to prepare himself for his mural decorations, he had done these trial works, which are described in his letters to Frédéric Villot. Reproductions of the three frescoes were published for the first time, I think, in M. Moreau-Nélaton's book. He does note that the subjects are drawn from Greek legends and that Delacroix had felt the antique world's love of the nude; but one finds no other observation as to the bond between the modern master's mentality and that of the ancients. It was only in 1927, when M. Escholier's second volume appeared, that we could read a fuller passage on this subject; its clearness of insight deserves for it a complete quotation.

After having spoken of the frescoes as "very Pompeiian in accent," the author says: "It was in Morocco that Eugène Delacroix made his new discovery of ancient life, the dignity of its draperies, the nobility of its attitudes; but it was at Valmont that, for the first time, his studies at the British Museum, his wonderful drawings from the Greek coins in the Blacas collection, and his notes from Tangier and Meknez give their whole fruit. Antiquity, which, from his childhood until his death, this humanist never ceased cherishing, antiquity appeared to him from that moment as a living person. In the *Leda,* the *Bacchus,* and the *Anacreon,* there is already the tremble of that antique life that was sought for in vain by Poussin, David, and Ingres. Admirable examples of it were to be offered by the Palais Bourbon and the Senate chamber of the Luxembourg, as also in the *Marcus Aurelius* and the *Trajan.* How easily can one imagine Eugène Delacroix, between two of the frescoes and obsessed with Rome and Athens, sending this line to Frédéric Villot: "I applaud you heartily for loving antiquity: it is the source of everything."

Now, the fact that Delacroix never set foot on the soil of Italy or of Greece, reveals the importance of that capital "obsession," if we want thus to characterize his classicism. Far from being the effect of that futile imitation against which we have heard his laughing raillery, his relationship with the ancient painters flows from a conception of art parallel with theirs. However, it seems impossible that works so near the antique as the *Leda,* the *Bacchus,* and the *Anacreon* at Valmont were not based on something more concrete than intuition. Neither the letters to Villot nor such information as I have been able to get from the critics most attentive to the problem of Delacroix indicate, notwithstanding, what source he followed—if there was one.

The collection of the Duc de Blacas, which I have mentioned, contained no antique paintings. Those which were in the Louvre at Delacroix's time (the fragments from that same Villa Boscoreale were not yet there) are of a quality far too weak to reveal to him the beauty of pictorial art as known to the ancients. The examples visible in his time would explain, indeed, this fragment of a phrase that he wrote in 1854, "the third-class daubs which still decorate the walls of Herculaneum." M. Escholier's words about the master's studies at the British Museum are not based on the *Journal* or the *Letters,* for these two sources of information are silent as to a possible contact with classical painting in London where, however, he drew from Greek statues.

Two possibilities remain open to us. In his will, Delacroix says of the Baronne de Forget: "She will be so kind as to receive back the volume she lent me of the *Antiquities of Herculaneum.*" Madame de Forget, whose family was connected with his own, had been a lifelong friend of his, therefore it is not at all impossible to think that the volume he speaks of was already in his possession when he painted the three frescoes at Valmont, and that the illustrations of the volume furnished him with his subjects. Almost more probable, although devoid of any sure foundation, is the idea for which I am greatly obliged to M. André Joubin, who suggested to me an inquiry as to the painter and rich collector who is always mentioned by his contemporaries as M. Auguste. A book by Ernest Chesneau informs us that this Jules-Robert Auguste, winner of the Prix de Rome in 1810, was a friend of Géricault's in Italy and that, on his return to France, his mementos of travel and his advice were very much appreciated by the group that gathered around him.

Ten years before the trials of fresco at Valmont, the *Journal* contained this note: "Dined with M. Auguste. Discussing his superb sketches of Neapolitan tombs, he speaks of the novel character one could give to religious subjects by inspiring oneself from the mosaics of the time of Constantine." The sketches from Naples may well have been lent to Delacroix later on, in the same way as other documents which M. Auguste had the habit of furnishing him for his pictures.

A last detail will exhaust the list of these sources of Delacroix's classical material. In 1844, he was preparing an article on the *Andromeda* of Puget and he noted in the *Journal:* "I must extract *in extenso* and cite the judgment of M. Eméric-David in the *Ephémérides*." We recall that Barye, that other great Romantic master, drew from Eméric-David the theory that the Greek artists had a system of anatomical measurements as the basis for their marvelous proportions, a system that Barye tried to recover by measuring the sculptures in the Louvre at the time of his curatorship there; we recall the studies in common of the great sculptor and the great painter, and from this standpoint the communication by the former to the latter of the ideas due to the archeologist seems extremely probable. Although a whole essay would be needed to demonstrate the basis of antique calm on which the fiery art of Barye reposes, it is useful to remark in passing that the sculptor of the *Theseus* figures had received the counsel of Gros, as his contemporary in painting had done, and that, in consequence, he descended from Louis David and from all that generation who had seen the fire of the classics rekindled in the days when the excavations at Pompeii revealed its splendor to the astonished eighteenth century.

Barye and Delacroix rejected the literal forms which the first classicists offered to art; and so the two younger men seemed revolutionaries to the weaklings of the period. But the whole lives of Barye and Delacroix denote a love for the classical spirit, a love which grew constantly more profound.

As proof—a thousand times more eloquent than all researches into our painter's relationship with the antique—is a picture dating from 1862 (see Plate 8), the year preceding the death of Delacroix. Three other paintings (not reproduced) complete one of his decorative ensembles. They are almost unknown in France since the time (about 1875) when they ceased to belong to Emile de Girardin.[1]

Since then, in New York, they continued to give their magisterial comment on the Pompeiian paintings in the museum of that city. The panther that Bacchus tames at Valmont (see Plate 7) reappears, almost thirty years later, before the chariot of the god. That is impressive, but we enter on another category of ideas when we see the way that the human race preserves the memory of its distant past if we consider how much of the figure of Bacchus himself recalls the masculine body of the antique fresco (see Plate 11) which the French master had never seen. Among the other canvases now at São Paulo, Diana and her nymphs seem to us, after looking at the paintings from *Magna Graecia*, of such beauty that, for an instant, the centuries are abolished and we have the illusion that this picture, so modern ninety-odd years ago (and indeed so modern still), is by a master of the ancient time. *Juno Imploring Aeolus* evokes for us the cadences of Homer so dear to Delacroix, even as Goethe, when an old man, was made to see again the images of *Faust* he formed in his youth; they recurred to him when he saw the drawings with which our artist, Parisian though he was, had just illustrated the poem. And if, from two heads of women in these frescoes of a later era, one can form an idea of what they could have been in the great period of such painting (a period not too far back since it must have followed that of the masterpieces of sculpture), should one imagine

1. The Robaut catalogue remarks: "Public opinion designates these four canvases as having been retouched by a different hand." To the doubtful authority of that "public opinion" one can oppose the confident words of M. Paul Durand-Ruel; he owned the four pictures for a long time and, many years after he had ceased to have any financial interest in them, affirmed that he had never been able to see in them a touch which was not from the hand of Delacroix. The pictures are now at the museum of São Paulo, Brazil, a fact which does little credit to our country—their host for over fifty years.

anything very different from *The Sibyl with the Golden Bough* (see Plate 9) by Delacroix?

I think that we may resume with profit the idea expressed in summary fashion by M. André Suarès at the time of the wonderful Ingres exhibition of 1911. He observed the apparent contradiction between two facts: whereas Ingres is regarded as the chief of the Classical School, all modern painting in his France with its tenacious traditions, comes forth from Delacroix. The fact is that the classical heritage which passed through the hands of men like Poussin, Corot, and Renoir caused the moderns to recognize that a more integral recalling of the beauties of the antique was the privilege of the man who, while pursuing the great Romantic adventure (the supreme adventure of artists in all periods) had never ceased to listen to the inner voice which told him of the treasure of his ancestors. That is why, ten years before his death, he closed his essay on Poussin, the classic of the seventeenth century, with the quotation from Reynolds which reads: "No modern picture so much resembles the paintings of the ancients as do those of Poussin." The man who copied that sentence as the finest of all praise knew how to understand its significance. And therefore his chapel at Saint-Sulpice becomes, for Cézanne and Redon, for Seurat and Signac, for Matisse and Derain, what the chapel of Masaccio was for the artists of Florence.

3

The Classicism of Barye

AT THE TIME OF THE EXHIBITION IN THE LOUVRE OF THE WORK OF Eugène Delacroix (1930), I tried to make clear in an article that element which had hardly been recognized in the master's art—his classicism. A critic taking issue with my article and writing in *Arte* of Turin (September, 1931), treated a nymph by Corot as an *académie,* adding that to class this painter among the adepts of classical landscape would be "an error comparable with an attempt to consider Delacroix as classical—an enterprise which, to tell the truth, was attempted recently." It is possible that my insufficient study of figures whose sole interest is academic blinds me to traces of the quality of Corot, and I shall never have the temerity to defend him against this criticism. But having, in 1930, associated Barye with Delacroix in my affirmation of the classical quality they have in common, I return to this thesis with a document which, it seems to me, touches very closely on the question.

In the collection of M. Jacques Zoubaloff, whose magnificent liberality enriched the Louvre with works by Barye, there was formerly a painting by the master which is here reproduced. To see it in a room with a cast from a certain Greek bronze of the end of the fifth century, B.C., in the Museum Antiker Kleinkunst in Munich, is to be struck by the resemblance between the two works. Was it the chance of an identical pose taken by two models during periods separated by more than two thousand years? Was it the result of a desire of Barye's to set himself, in painting, the same problem of form which he had observed in the Greek sculpture? Both hypotheses exclude themselves equally. That pose, one of the easiest for a model to take, has been rendered by draftsmen, painters, and sculptors many thousands of times without suggesting a relationship with the bronze at Munich. Chance has therefore no more to do with the question than in the other cases: a logical reason is the one we want to find. And, as to a direct influence, the possibility simply does not exist, for the good reason that the bronze had not yet been unearthed during Barye's lifetime. From information very courteously furnished me by Professor Sieveking, the director of the classical collections of Munich who first published this bronze,[2] it was discovered by him in the excavations at Beroia, near Salonica, in 1909 (Barye died in 1875).

Whence, then, does this resemblance come? It comes from the same source which led to the perfect harmony between the paintings of Delacroix's last years and Greek painting, represented by the frescoes of Pompeii which I reproduced in 1930. In their presence one understood at once why the cross-hatching of the artists of *Magna Graecia* was infallibly recognized in its kinship with modern art by persons familiar with Delacroix's use of the procedure. The case is the one which we frequently see in science, when two men in different countries, but basing themselves on the same ideas, arrive independently at an identical solution of a problem. More significant yet was the fact that Delacroix, who had never visited Italy or Greece, had a mind impregnated with classical culture to such a degree that his art prolonged that of the ancients and caused the unmistakable resemblance between his *The Sibyl with the Golden Bough* and that woman of the Boscoreale fresco which the excavations down to his lifetime had not yet even brought to daylight.

Is it not the same relationship that we are now seeing between the

---

2. In the *Münchener-Jahrbuch der Bildenden Kunst,* Bd. V (1910), p. 1; then in the *Deutschen Archaeologischen Jahrbuch,* Bd. 25 (1910), p. 481.

Barye and the Greek bronze? As has been said, it is not the pose of the model which produces in our minds the identity of feeling we have in the presence of the two works. Suppose some one says that all he sees is a nude woman when looking at this modern painting: I imagine he would hesitate to confess that his conception of the ancient masterpiece was dominated by thoughts of her sex, for she has at times been called a *hetaira,* a "pleasure girl." On the contrary, considerations from the realm of plastics, qualities like equilibrium and harmony are the essentials, and proportion—in its aspect of a thing nearer to architecture than to merely anatomical measurements. Unless one takes refuge in the external resemblance of the pose, one is therefore compelled to admit that the bond between the two figures is their aesthetic quality.

Have we given enough attention to what Roger Ballu says when, in his big book on Barye, he mentions the fact that the sculptor, as a curator at the Louvre, took the measurements of the statues there— not on rare occasions but hundreds of times, comparing the proportions thus obtained from antique, Renaissance, and modern sculptures? Have we sufficiently meditated the meaning of such study for a man of Barye's implacable exactitude, a man who had tested Eméric-David's affirmation that Greek sculpture was based on a mathematical canon of the proportions? Does anyone want to believe that the relationship between the head by Barye in his *Theseus Killing the Minotaur* and the heads in archaic Greek works is a thing of chance? Or is it not infinitely more reasonable, in the presence of these facts, to conclude that there was a rebirth of the classical spirit in the artist whom Ledru-Rollin, in 1848, had named chief of the casting studio at the Louvre and curator of the Gallery of Plaster Models? He worked at his own sculpture in the museum, in the very presence of the Greek figures, and we know that it was in the Louvre that he had created a group designed to serve as a pendant to that *Centaur and Lapith* which, on the monument of the Ile St. Louis, has made of that site a place of pilgrimage for the best artists of our time.[3]

It is not a mark of humility on my part if I retire from the discussion here and offer as the finest proof of Barye's classicism the effect which he produced on two great literary artists.

Théophile Gautier (quoted by Charles Saunier in his excellent

---

3. This is, unhappily, no longer true, the great sculpture having been yielded to the Germans to melt into metal in the Second World War.

study of Barye) wrote of the sculpture which we have just recalled: "The *Centaur Overcome by a Lapith* shows that this Romantic, proscribed by juries, was the modern master of statuary who most closely approached Phidias and Greek Sculpture. This Lapith, with his robust and simple forms, beautiful as the ideal, true as nature, could have figured on the front of the Parthenon, by the side of the Ilyssus, and the centaur could have mingled with the cavalcade of the metopes."

Let us hear how Théophile Silvestre reports on the technical procedures that he had observed in the studio of Barye—the flexible armatures, for example: "If he perceives that his figure is, at a certain place, sinning against the laws of statics or of anatomy, nothing prevents his correcting it. See also how his groups are turned, set into perspective and made to stand upright, from whatever side you examine them. I have no need to speak of the style: if they were in marble and bore traces of the injuries wrought by time, one would say that they had been detached from the Parthenon. Barye did not, however, imitate the Greeks, but nature made him an Athenian."

And there is the key to the mystery. That man who, with Delacroix, best incarnated the new aspiration of the nineteenth century, the man in whose work the adversaries of Darwin thought to see an attempt to justify the theories as to animals of the English savant, bears in his genius the heritage of the greatest art of the past. An "Athenian," Barye rejoins his brother of the ancient time who bequeathed to us the sculpture in Munich, and yet he remains himself in this painting, as he is in the work saluted by the writers we have just reread.

M. Paul Jamot, after studying the French exhibition in London (1931), wrote that the configuration of the countries colonized by the Greeks in France recalled to them their "dear Hellas," and from this resemblance he passed on to a kinship of the mind. This new example of Barye's work would not be one of the least to support the thesis.

4

Some Notes on Delacroix

THE SUBJECT TREATED IN THIS ARTICLE, THOUGH A RETURN TO SOME
ideas of over twenty years ago (see Chapter 2), will never, one may
affirm, lose its interest. For, of the multiple elements characterizing the
arts, there is not one of greater importance than that which permits us
to understand the degree to which the masters accept the teachings of
the past and, together with that, the role of new creation; or, to use
words authorized by many learned men, the classical element and the
romantic element. In general, criticism has preferred to recognize, in
the case of Eugène Delacroix, the predominance of romanticism, doing
so in spite of the fact that in an exchange of words often quoted, the
master—when hearing a comparison between Berlioz and himself—
sharply declared: "You are mistaken, sir, I am a pure classicist." A
willful paradox? That is something I have never admitted, and now
less than ever, for it is with material proof that I reopen the question,
a proof I had sought for in vain before publishing my first article on
the subject. That was in 1930, at the time of the great exhibition in

the Louvre, when an incomparable retrospective of Delacroix crowned the three-year celebration accorded to the Centenary of romanticism. The director of *L'Amour de l'Art* at that time, M. François Fosca, considered that no phase of the mentality of the great painter save his classicism demanded so urgently to be brought out; and, noting the examples of it that I could furnish him, he entrusted me with the theme for the June issue of that same year.

The article stirred up opposition, notably from the Italian review, *Arte,* which treated my thesis almost like an attempt to get effect at a low price: to say that Delacroix possessed the classical qualities—and to a high degree—was for an Italian writer the act of a man who wanted to attract attention to himself by saying that black was white.

In reply, *L'Amour de l'Art,* November, 1932, published two photographs, one of a Greek masterpiece and the other of a painting by Barye, who occupies a position very near to that of Delacroix, for the two masters have about the same placing as regards romanticism. Now, the work by Barye resembled the Greek work to such an extent that one was very tempted to think of a direct imitation; yet the modern had never seen the ancient sculpture, since it had not been revealed by excavation until thirty-four years after his death; this proof of a genius common to a Greek and a Frenchman (a matter already pointed out by Théophile Gautier and Théophile Silvestre, as I mentioned before) is all the more striking—and the more precious—for people who believe in the permanence of the fundamental elements of the arts.

This aspect of the discussion still seems to me the essential thing about the problem; nonetheless, a sufficient number of students will be interested by a new example of parallelism between the art always accepted as classical and the one to which so many persons are unwilling to attribute any other quality than romanticism. It is true that in the present case we are in the presence of an almost direct borrowing by Delacroix from Pompeiian painting. (Let us recall that this art is not admired merely because it is our only example, in any considerable quantity, of ancient painting, but because it is really Greek: the artists who came from Alexandria and who worked in Campania brought with them ideas and processes which we see in the museums to have been transmitted from Greece to Egypt, and then to Italy.) But since, down to the present time, we lacked concrete testimony of a relationship between the great Romantic and the painting of the Greeks, we shall proceed without further preface to our documentation.

The drawing by Delacroix, *Centauress and Bacchante,* (see Plate 15), has been for twenty years an inexhaustible source of pleasure for me. The delicacy of shading, due to the use of a quite hard pencil, serves only to emphasize the grandeur of the general conception which, today, takes on a new importance since it derives from that Pompeiian fresco (Plate 14), which we submit to our readers. (This fresco, with three others of a similar nature, is designated by the number 9,133 in the catalogue of the Museo Nazionale of Naples. They come from the villa called "Cicero's.") It was to illustrate our article that this painting was photographed, thanks to the kindness of Professor Mario Napoli, curator at the Museo Nazionale. The very limited dimensions and the modest coloration of this picture explain why it is rarely reproduced. But Delacroix's drawing proves that it was thought of in a different way at the time when a volume of engravings from the *Antiquities of Herculaneum* was published—and reached the hands of the French master. (We may take note, since the fresco in question comes from Pompeii and not from Herculaneum, that the names of the two cities were used almost indiscriminately, one for the other, in the eighteenth century and for a long time afterward.)

We know with certainty that Delacroix possessed this collection, for, as I have mentioned, in his will he asked his executors to return it to the Baronne de Forget who had had the kindness to lend it to him. The fact that Delacroix was so conscientiously concerned with the volume at the moment when he foresaw his imminent death, shows how much he appreciated the value of the loan. Since he never realized any of his divers projects of a trip to Italy, and since the little fresco has never been in France, we have the certitude that it was from an engraving that the master executed the present drawing; indeed, it is superfluous to point out that the position of the figures is reversed in Delacroix's drawing. His careful observation of the details and a special sobriety in the technique are exactly what one might expect in a drawing from one of those old engravings whose purpose was to reproduce the subject with the maximum of fidelity.

Thus is dissipated the mystery of a theme unknown anywhere else in the work of the painter. The suggestion of a friend who had imagined this drawing to be one of the multiple researches leading up to the *Education of Achilles* in the Chamber of Deputies, does not, however, lose its interest. On the contrary, those who see a special success in this masterpiece among the pendentives of the Palais Bourbon have no cause for complaint when it turns out that their favorite composition has, as its probable base, a classical fresco. The paintings which are the great ornament of the Library of the Chamber of Deputies date from the years 1844-46. If our drawing dates before that time, it would indeed be a long while that Delacroix had kept the precious volume which his relative had confided to him—unless he had given it back previously and then asked for it again toward the end of his life. While recognizing the difficulty of dating a reproductive drawing, I had always inclined toward the old age of the master for the period of the *Centauress*. It was in 1862, the year before his death, that he executed his finest replica of the scene with Achilles and the centaur, Chiron, the one in the collection of the Marquise de Ganay. Another version of the subject, a pastel of very high quality, dating from the same period and now in an American collection, proves how much this antique scene, imagined twenty years before, preoccupied the master during his last months.

That offers one reason more for rejoicing over this new testimony to the survival of the classical instinct in France. In the humble workman with a neglected education, as Barye was at his beginnings, we see the intuition of Greek beauty triumphing over his lack of acquaintance with the marvelous sculpture evoked by his picture. His early comrade, Delacroix, was the son of a Minister of State and an ambassador of France who had caused him to be instructed in the "good humanities" cited by Cézanne as characterizing the education of the period. And so one sees again that love for the classical which, until the end of the master's life, caused him to meditate on the surest sources of European inspiration.

5

The Later Masters

WHEN WE READ ABOUT THÉOPHILE GAUTIER AND THÉOPHILE SILVESTRE invoking supreme achievements of the human race in their defense of a modern in a previous chapter, it would have been easy to think that the genius of the two writers was enough to bring about a definitive agreement. But that is not the case. Nearly a hundred years after the death of Delacroix, the biting phrase of Degas still applies to him, "the cheapest of the great masters." (I need not say that Degas' loving search for Delacroix works to add to his collection excludes any derogatory meaning to his word "cheapest.")

And as to Barye, my own unhappy description of him is, "the man nobody knows." Half a year ago, an eminent Italian publisher wrote asking me for an article on Corot to be part of an encyclopedia of art. I replied that though I had a fervent admiration for Corot, I thought I might better write on Barye, since I had studied him particularly. The publisher decided on both articles, adding a request that the one on Barye be done immediately since the volume of names beginning with *B* was already in print. That meant that the encyclopedia would have lacked all mention of the greatest modern sculptor had I not made my suggestion.

The case is an extreme one, but we cannot be reminded too often that fundamental matters are disregarded time after time by people in power if, indeed, they ever knew how valid was the rank which authorities had united in according to a given artist. To take the opposite case: no one of standing, as far as I can learn, has ever said so much as a good word for Dali's *Crucifixion,* and yet it continues to hang on the walls of America's greatest museum, despite the protests which appeared in the press from the time when it was first shown. One of the artists who then wrote against it had made what turned out, unexpectedly, to be the prophetic idea of comparing it to *September Morn,* that pitiful academic nude which had only its slick painting to suggest linking it with the *Crucifixion.* But no, the Metropolitan remained consistent with itself in its first blunder by acquiring *September Morn.* It was made "the picture of the month," and was touted by the museum as "one of the most controversial works of modern times"—which it was not, for the record proves that its reputation for immorality and its consequent banishment from the mails was merely the work of a publisher who, by his own statement, later on, said he had made eighty thousand dollars from the sale of reproductions. The trickery through which he induced Anthony Comstock to denounce the work was nowhere near the level of real controversy.

But perhaps a more flagrant case of the museum's disregard for established values is to be seen in the words used by the director, Francis Henry Taylor, to boost the sculptures by Carl Milles. Of the Swedish artist whose *Fountain of the Muses* had just appeared in the Metropolitan, Mr. Taylor, writing in the official *Bulletin* of the museum for January, 1956, tells that Milles "was at home in the classical world to a degree that no other artist of our time has ever been." (No wonder that Barye is the forgotten man.) In the next paragraph one reads: "The trolls and sprites of Peer Gynt talked with him on equal terms with nymphs and hamadryads of Olympus and Helicon." I have too high a regard for Ibsen's *Peer Gynt* to believe that the trolls and sprites reported faithfully on the great Northern fantasies. As for the lovely creatures of the Greek woods and streams, they never got a word

in, or if they did, it was all Greek to Milles. Making every allowance
for the adulteration by Rome of the beauty obtained by the older
civilization, Mr. Taylor adds insult to injury when he describes Milles
in his studio at the American Academy in Rome, "drinking in the sunset on the Seven Hills and peopling his mind with gods and goddesses
of antiquity."

The injury I just mentioned consisted in placing in our museum
those ridiculous gods and goddesses (not of antiquity but of a modern
man, alien in race and thought to the antique); to bolster them up
with the sunset fancies of the aging sculptor is to accuse the reader of
having no sense at all of the classical values.

Enough of these passing aberrations! We may now approach the
solid elements in our subject, the unbroken succession of artists who
do continue the qualities bequeathed us by the classics of the past. It
will not be necessary to go into such detail as we have given to Delacroix and Barye. That was justified by the position of the two great
men, standing as they do so near the threshold of modern art, and
representing to the fullest degree that school of romanticism which
was at first looked on as opposed to the classical; I assume we are agreed
that they both give the most authoritative testimony in favor of the
classical.

How natural that they should do so! On the soil from which they
sprang the classics had reflowered with the purity which makes us catch
our breath each time we see *The Rivers of France* (see Plate 3) on the
fountain of Jean Goujon. Or take his *Diana* in the Louvre (it is only
of recent years that extreme prudence in attribution has led the museum to label it merely "French School"). When we compare it with
Cellini's *Diana,* in a nearby room, we are utterly convinced that the
French work is far nearer than the Italian to Greek sources.

Such also is our idea of Poussin's *The Realm of Flora* (see Plate 4).
The young Norman, who had had to make such strenuous efforts to
get to Rome, looked with humility on what he found in the Renaissance capital. Around him were decadents of the schools of Michelangelo and Raphael. He has very little in common with their facile
technique and their Baroque use of space relations. Copying four times
over the *Aldobrandini Wedding* of a late Greek artist, and prayerfully
drawing the bas-reliefs on Roman sarcophagi, he is immeasurably
nearer the classical past than to the Carracci clan or to such near-

contemporaries as Guido Reni and Guercino. It would of course be excessive to say that the Italians' familiarity with the ancient art they saw everywhere had had its usual effect of breeding contempt, but Guercino, for instance, was soon to be influenced by Caravaggio's stark naturalism, whereas Poussin said that Caravaggio came into the world to destroy the art of painting.

It is the Frenchmen, Claude Lorrain, in landscape as Poussin with the figure, who bring back the classical values, as we see anew in the following century, when Watteau (see Plate 5), from the Flemish part of France and formed by an older Fleming (Rubens), rounds out the supremacy of classical art among the French.

The Revolution, for all its violence, only confirms such an idea. David goes back to Greco-Roman art for inspiration and makes it the foundation-stone of his school, with its long-continued influence; even the Cubists invoke its rigorous logic and discipline a century later. No wonder, when *The Sabines* contains such passages of classical beauty (see Plate 6), that we forget the painter's political theories.

The writings of Lessing and Winckelmann, among others, the excitement over the discoveries at Pompeii, and the exhaustion of the eighteenth century's exquisite genius, all contributed to make an art based on the classics the really modern art of the time. Delacroix's very romantic enthusiasm for what he saw in Morocco was to remain with him undiminished until the end of his life; and two years after his historic visit to the Near East, he painted a masterpiece of instinct with classical balance, the *Women of Algiers;* and yet, in that same year, 1834, when he prepared for his first series of murals in the Chamber of Deputies, he did not turn for inspiration to the Orient, but addressed himself to classical sources in the frescoes at Valmont. Such a conception as theirs appeared to him the most suitable for work in the great tradition of the walls—of architecture; and he adhered to classical themes and treatment throughout his mural work, right down to his last fully completed decorations at St. Sulpice (see Plate 12) where he did not hesitate to invite comparison with Raphael (see Plate 13). It is with even greater freedom, but still from classical subjects and with profoundly classical design, that he undertook the glorious (if slightly unfinished) decorations at the museum of São Paulo, Brazil (see Plate 8).

As to these last and finest of his monumental compositions, I trust

that my preceding pages will give the reader some explanation for
seeing in them an example—indeed the supreme one—of the classical
genius that informs the art of Delacroix. But there is a phase of it
which has received no more than a hint until now—it is that capacity
of the master for the impersonal, generalizing character as is seen in
Greek heads. I referred to it back in 1930 when associating in character
the head of that *Woman with a Shield* (see Plate 10) from Boscoreale
and the noble features of Delacroix's *The Sibyl with the Golden Bough*
(see Plate 9). Both have the ethic (as contrasted with the pathetic)
quality that we find in the most classical period of Greek sculpture.
The two adjectives denote feeling: but ethic treats it in a way to in-
volve all of mankind, whereas individual feeling results in what the
Greek referred to as *pathos*. Thus it is a late art, that which arose at
Alexandria, which gives us the startlingly individual portraits of the
Fayum; and a similar masterpiece from Pompeii, *The Baker and His
Wife* (see Plate 29). *The Woman with a Shield,* on the other hand,
looks back to the impersonal triumphs of the *ethos,* and it is fitting to
note how its quality continues in Delacroix, who cared little for portrait painting.

Yet he had the strongest feeling for Rembrandt, who penetrates so
profoundly to humanity's romantic depths and, among the men of
Delacroix's own time, he is influenced by Gros whose *Self Portrait*
(see Plate 28), Rembrandtesque and romantic in unmistakable
fashion, is almost a confession of heresy to the neo-classic principles of
David, his revered master.

Perhaps we may see the explanation of Gros' suicide in his in-
ability to keep to the letter of those severe rules which David laid down
for his school. Delacroix recognized the great stature of "the restorer
of the French school" as he called David; like Géricault—also a deep
admirer of the painter of the Revolution, like Barye and the other
strong young men, he played his immense part in the romantic movement of which Gros is to be considered the initiator—paying with his
life for the privilege, if my analysis of his despair during his last years
is correct. The tragedy deepens when we consider the pride and vin-
dication that Gros ought to have felt had he realized the share he had
in such triumphs as Géricault's *Raft of the Medusa* and Delacroix's
Dante and Virgil. As the first teacher of Barye, Gros was entitled to
deep satisfaction in that artist's *Lapith and Centaur,* which we have

heard acclaimed by two master critics. It contains much that may well have been inspired by Gros in his magnificent *Prince Yussupof on Horseback* and his other equestrian portraits. Their classical source of ideas was behind Delacroix in his fascination (by way of a mere engraving) with the *Centauress and Bacchante* from Pompeii, a feeling which continues in him not only during his work at the Chamber of Deputies but down to the year before his death when he produced one more version of his *Achilles and the Centaur* (see Plate 16); it must have been one of the works he preferred.

My Paris article of 1948 contains the ideas I have at present as to Plates 17, 18, and 19, but I should like to add some comment on the works by Barye not previously discussed.

The *Three Graces* (see Plate 20), is so classical in subject that its authorship by the chief sculptor of romanticism may cause astonishment to people who know him only as "the animal man." But there is a point to observe that has special significance in considering Barye's relationship to the Greeks. Their famous group of the *Three Graces*, piously accepted by Raphael in his small picture at Chantilly, shows us the three young women as separate figures: had one of them got tired of posing, she could have walked away. Not so with the figures in Barye's group: their lines and volumes interlace for all the after-time. They form an entity as indissoluble as that of the two beings united in the Sphinx of Egypt, or the various components—man, lion, bull, and eagle of Assyrian sculpture, and give one more example of the broadness of base which classicism had in the nineteenth century.

As time went on, this base widened further through contact with arts previously unknown. Ingres and Manet, Van Gogh and Whistler, to name very diverse artists, testified to the beauty of Japanese prints—by their words or their work, or by both. The classical concept of design underwent modification upon contact with the art of a people strongly attached to traditions of its own, but accessible to Europeans also. Then, when Matisse, Picasso, and the rest discovered the art of the African Negro, new elements again were added to our resources. While a romantic feeling for the supernatural was the dominating force in African art, the Cubists were quick to see in it an architecture of planes (often similar in effect to what the Romanesque offers us), and Picasso and Braque used such a structural conception for their works of 1910 and the next few years. The ideas of the Africans, the romantic side of their art, being of no use to Europeans, the living geometry of the Negroes, the classical in their art, was taken over eagerly by the Cubists in their discontent with what they regarded as the lack of form in the Impressionists.

Finally, in this brief review of the influences which have broadened our range of the classical qualities, we come to the art of the ancient Mexicans. As yet it has been intelligently used by only a few men among their descendants, but the extended and rapid growth of appreciation that we are witnessing for the sculpture of the Olmecs, the Toltecs, the Aztecs, and the others is proof of the wisdom shown by Diego Rivera in his reply to an American art teacher; she had asked him whether the training of our students should stress consideration of the classics. "Decidedly it should," answered Rivera, "they should give deep study to the classics—*our* classics." Probably he was thinking of the great things of ancient America, but the wide inclusiveness of his own research in Europe prevents anyone's imagining that he would reject attention to the classics of Greece, Italy, France, and other countries.

Since I have been emphasizing for so long the classical aspect of art, perhaps this is the moment to warn against the error of partisanship for either of the two schools. The romantic is, as I have said, a necessary complement for the classical, as we see if we take note of the fact that this is not just a matter of theory but of experience. No great work can be found devoid of a romantic or of a classical strain. As an example, let us observe Barye's *Jaguar and Hare* (see Plate 21), one of his masterpieces. The intense observation of the big cat as it quivers with the enjoyment of its victim's life-blood is so powerfully expressed that it is no wonder if, for the layman, this romantic phase of the work monopolizes his interest in the great sculpture. But the point is that this would not be a great sculpture, it would be merely a brutal document as to the fight for existence, if it were not unshakeably founded on classic harmony and perfection. Such qualities put it into an order of ideas radically different from those of the vast majority of animal sculptures. The sensations such things give us are those that we get from a visit to the zoo—only that in the latter case the impressions are so much stronger and more varied.

The line of beauty, the S shape insisted on by Hogarth, dominates the whole figure of the jaguar and, from the snarl of the features to

the twitch of the tail, every turn of line or plane contributes its in-
crease of effect to the concentrated movement of the ensemble. The
tragedy and triumph of nature translate themselves into the language
of art. Barye was right in his stern reply to his critics: he said that in
placing him on the level of the animals, his subjects, they placed themselves below the beasts. The falsification deriving from a confusion of
subject and significance is however so common that we shall never
purge it from the public mind. Yet once one has felt the beauty of such
a work as Barye's water color of the *Leopard Resting* (see Plate 22),
hope returns again that there will be general enjoyment of such noble
things.

Turning now to Ingres, I feel an impulse to ask pardon of his shade
for associating him with men like Géricault and Delacroix whom he
denounced so bitterly during his lifetime. But who can affirm that in
the Elysian Fields, where he has dwelt since, he has not mellowed and
that he sees that the truth may be reached from one point of the com-
pass as well as another. His own line of approach was through drawing, as everyone knows. But do we all see that even his consummate
mastery here was a matter of line, and that the spaces between the lines
were filled with a type of "shading" which led his contemporaries to
the cruel anagram of his name, making it say "in gray"—*en gris.* He
abhorred Rubens whose radiant spaces were at the poles from his own.
Miraculous as were his contours, Ingres's color was often slatey or dis-
cordant when isolated or unrelated tones were juxtaposed. As for the
sculptor's modeling, that which associates the form with surrounding
space and varies that form as it recedes in perspective, the modeling
which leads from Michelangelo to Delacroix, I cannot think of a single
example of it in the work of Ingres. A figure or just a hand may stand
out—in the *Martyrdom of St. Symphorien,* for example—but it is always
a matter of black-and-white contrasts, though their boundary lines are
marvelous in their subtle adjustments.

We are brought back to Emerson's true words—that we do not love
men for absence of defects but for presence of virtues. Ingres merits the
epithet "divine" which George Moore applied to him, borrowing the
term from the master in his constant use of it for Raphael. But at once
the mention of the Italian brings us to a realization of how far apart
the two men were. Again, as with Poussin when compared with the
Bolognese, we feel the difference between the man born to share the

riches around him and the man who must achieve his purpose solely by his own effort. Raphael, beginning under Perugino with easy docility, goes on from one influence to another—even that of Michelangelo—without the tremble of an eyelash; he is as innocent in his borrowings from Leonardo and the others as he is in directing the many men in his workshop. As a result of this the experts of today are at a loss to say who painted what in a majority of his pictures.

How different is the modern time! Ingres himself affirmed that no one could copy his painting. Alongside the classical masters he followed so prayerfully, there had come into his work the romantic element of personality. It continues from his youth (the lovely *The Bather of Valpinçon*, Plate 23, dates from his twenty-eighth year) to his old age when, in his *Mme. Ingres* (see Plate 24), he achieves an amplitude, a breathless perfection, he had never reached before. Despite all his devotion to Raphael and the Greeks, can anyone say that pictures like the two just recalled are products of classical inspiration alone? No, Ingres' constant insistence that his pupils follow nature is seen here in its so lovable effect on his own work. What we must recognize is a romantic love for the beauty of the model in the *Bather* and for the superior woman who devoted herself to him in his last years. Here is one of the supreme cases of the uniting of the two great tendencies of art: Ingres—too often thought of as solely the classicist—achieves his greatest successes in works where the romantic quality enters in.

We must likewise change our earlier idea of Corot. What the Parisian dealers used to call the "Corot d'Amérique," fifty or seventy-five years ago, was almost certainly a landscape, preferably one of silvery tone and with some feathery trees. It was popular in this country because of our people's love of nature—in her milder forms, above all. Americans would not have resented the word *magot* (a clumsy, boorish person) which academic critics in France applied to the figure pieces of the master. It was reserved for a later generation of Americans to buy the *Hagar and Ishmael* (see Plate 25), a "historical landscape" far different in mood and technique from the romantic glimpses of sky and water that charmed an earlier public, eager for a new rendering of nature. Only with Constable and other Englishmen, a generation or so before Corot, had there been anything like the love of nature that we see in the great Dutch school, in Ruisdael above all. The discoverers of the Fontainebleau forest had a pantheist love of the out of doors easily appreciated by a people relatively naïve about art, as were the Americans of nearly a century ago, and so Théodore Rousseau with his almost religious fervor, Millet, Daubigny, and the rest could have their splendid success with our public. Corot could have such success also, without its being realized, either here or in France, that he had a classical quality not shared by any other of his group.

Millet had worked much at the Louvre, to be sure, and carried the result of his museum study into his painting at Barbizon. But how limited it appears when we look at the *Hagar and Ishmael,* or the pure figure pieces of Corot. To come at once to the most striking example of the matter, let us recall the sensation that thrilled Paris when *Woman With a Pearl* (see Plate 26) was added to the Louvre. Men vied with one another in admiration for the way a "landscapist" had handled the figure, and a portrait into the bargain. Finally Derain spoke the decisive word—that the new picture ought to be placed alongside the *Mona Lisa* (see Plate 27). Then people's eyes were opened. The contemporary painter had not been influenced in his judgment by the close similarity of the pose in the two models: he had revealed the essential likeness of the two works in their classical drawing, in the calm aloofness of their characterization, in the perfection of their form-relations and their space-relations. Corot, who had done as much as anyone for the modern attitude toward landscape, was seen to be in the most intimate line leading back to the Greeks.

Again as to Courbet: not many have read without surprise the passage in Redon's book where he speaks of the chieftain of realism as "that great classical artist." Yet a mere glance at the *Woman with a Parrot* (see Plate 30), for example, tells us how right Redon is in his allusion. We may have delighted in the work before, we may have enjoyed its celebration of the splendor of flesh, its sledge-hammer strength in sheer painting, and the originality with which the forms are disposed. But Redon's word opens up new vistas of understanding and, as we follow them, we have new satisfactions in realizing that our sensations were not merely casual or personal: they were the result of logical thinking.

That emboldens me to hope that the reader will not regard my constant harping on "romantic" and "classic" as the result of a fixed idea followed out willy-nilly, but as something which reveals funda-

mental aspects of art, and explains as few other things can, what makes
the particular value of this work or that. Many an error comes from
asking a painting or sculpture for qualities foreign (or almost so) to
what it is able to offer. The narrow even if marvelous classicism of
Ingres causes him to say unjust things not merely about the men of
his time, but about Signorelli, Rubens, and Rembrandt.

Or take the case of the early misunderstanding of Edouard Manet.
His teacher, Couture, doubtless had his unfaithful pupil at least par-
tially in mind when he painted his caricature of *The Realist*. It por-
trays a painter at work, a coarse peasant seated with his fat buttocks
directly on a Greek marble head, and staring at the source of his inspiration, a hog. I really have no basis for the supposition that the
realist in question was Manet, though after he exhibited his *Olympia*
the case was that of the old saying: "There's no stick so mean but you
can beat a dog with it." And had not Manet by turning Courbet's
painting from dark to light taken a new step in the direction of realism? Why, only a short time later, light was to be the chief preoccupation of the Impressionists! Well might Delacroix fulminate in his
Journal against the "accursed realist"! It is almost sure that he did not
have Courbet in mind for this since, on a nearby page, he expresses
admiration for the latter's talent and power.

But suppose that even *his* intelligence and culture had not served
him: the case would merely prove that no one is infallible. Couture
and the great majority who thought as he did were simply little men
making their futile attempt to hold on to the past and failing to see
that Manet, haunting the museums and copying there, carried his
classical tradition so naturally that he did not have to parade it, as does
the parvenu of culture. Thus the amazing clarity of the *Bar at the
Folies Bergères* (see Plate 31) goes back to Quatrocento Italy, indeed
to the glory of shadowless form in Piero della Francesca.

Was it this preoccupation with earlier times or was it an inherent
opposition to newcomers which caused Manet to utter disparaging
words about Renoir? Here, at least, we do have a case of bad misunderstanding of a younger master by an older one. And it is the more
surprising because Renoir is precisely the member of the Impressionist
group who was best fitted to build on Manet's innovations in form and
color. Can there be any doubt of this when we recall the *Mother and
Child* (see Plate 32) and see that the chief difference between it and

the late Manets is in an added fineness of sentiment? That does, to be sure, carry with it technical advances like the subtler conception of drawing and modeling, as well as a magic of color that goes beyond Manet's splendid observation and positivism.

A few years after the elder man's death, Renoir slowly reaches that pinnacle in his work, the *Girls Bathing* (see Plate 33). It is another triumphant meeting place of the romantic and classical qualities. Only in part emerging from the cocoon of Impressionism (it was later on that Renoir spoke out strongly against his early school) he still profits by the full gamut of its color. This had reached a climax, some five years before, in the *Boatmen Lunching* of the Phillips Gallery in Washington, but as we go from the one masterpiece to the other, we see how the severe study of drawing which had intervened was changing the character of the work. Renoir had recently come back from Italy, and if the dazzling light of Naples or Venice had led to a maximum effort to render luminosity by color, the most important effect of his seeing the Italian—and Pompeiian—classics was on his sense of form. Indeed so strong was his impression of the simple technique of the murals that for a time he was tempted by fresco painting and, though he speaks of his "great discovery" that oil painting is done with oil, there was still some memory of preparing the ground for fresco when the canvas for the *Girls Bathing* was primed.

At all events there is a special brilliance to the white underlying the colors of the radiant work. But, enchanting in color as it is, its chief virtues are in its design and its modeling. The adorable femininity of his models and our delight in the way they unite with the air and the sunshine are romantic elements in the picture's prodigious effect, but the enduring impression it leaves is of suave modeling, as fine as that in the Renaissance or even in the ancient works Renoir had studied in Italy.

Year after year, joyful work tells of the master's balanced development. Sometimes he seems to go on unconscious of problems, merely delighting in the hues of summer and flowers and the young people who concentrate on themselves all the surrounding beauty. At other times he is taking himself in hand to correct some excess or to reinforce some quality that promised further progress. At all events each decade —we almost could say each year—brings us to a higher level in his art. And so, with all the wonder of the two canvases of the eighties that we

have seen, the *Two Women with Flowered Hats* (see Plate 34) of 1915
is still more of a miracle. (Incidentally, it is here reproduced for the
first time.)

In the sense that all real art is inexplicable, any first rate work is a
thing of magic—the word losing all connection with superstition or the
like. You can go into enchanted admiration for the way life informs
every bit of this late Renoir, the hints of foliage as well as the full-
blooded young bodies; even the draperies and the hats are part of the
Ode to Joy formed by the picture as a whole. Or, in a studious and
analytical mood you can put a sheet of tracing paper over the reproduction and, with a pencil, follow the composition of pyramids which
results from following the great masses as they move to and fro. You
were at first dealing with the romantic, lyrical elements in the work;
but then even if an investigation of its classical control of form does
give you an added satisfaction as to your understanding, be assured
that you have not advanced a hair's breadth toward arriving at the way
the miracle was performed. Nothing made Renoir more nervous and
impatient than attempts to find a *modus operandi* for his work—and
that of other artists.

He was of a generation and, above all, of a temperament that dis-
trusted analysis and needed no more than inspiration from nature and
the fructifying sunlight of art to do his beautiful work. But the latter
years of the nineteenth century brought with them a new consciousness
of the complexity of art, and men like Gauguin, Van Gogh, and Seurat
asked more and more searching questions as to what differentiates an
aesthetic performance from the mere tricks of reproducing appearances.

The man who seemed to offer the most of logic in his building of
the picture was Cézanne, and soon it was by the thousands that paintings derived from landscapes and still lifes like those here illustrated
(see Plates 36 and 37) were produced. To be sure, Cézanne's personal
greatness was an important influence on the later men, but his work
had also a legibility, a possibility of being analyzed and understood in
its structure, that made him particularly serviceable to the younger
men. Thus in the works where he is most frank in showing how he
develops his initial idea, his effect on his followers is most clearly seen.
Very often such works are the water colors and, from such a one as is
offered here (see Plate 38), one sees how easy was the progression to
cubism. First Derain with his stressing of the planes, which turn like a

door on its hinges, and then Picasso and Braque, with their fragmentation and recomposition of the planes, arrive at the new structure of pictorial space already implicit in the more naturalistic conception of Cézanne.

If the master had to wait longer for recognition by the public than anyone else of his group, at least he had the satisfaction, at an early time, of knowing that he had deep appreciation from artists—and the best of them. It was natural that a Renoir or a Claude Monet should find favor before he did. The romantic qualities are always admired first, in this case the feminine beauty of Renoir's models and, with Monet, the brilliance of the light. The classical qualities would appeal to artists first of all, so that the decisive voice of the professionals often needs a certain time before it is heard. In a painting like *The Clock-maker* (see Plate 35), the two elements of art are held in perfect balance. From the human standpoint the work ranks with the great masterpieces of character rendering: the man is so deeply understood that he is a symbol of all men. From the standpoint of aesthetic organization, the picture is impeccable. It is a little late to draw up a list of the beauties in a Cézanne, but on the other hand, since he gave so much attention to things like the rhythmical structure in the details of the coat and the adjustment of planes in the head, I want to say I think the awesome grandeur of the picture as a whole derives from its proportions; they have their origin in things like the figures on Athenian tombs. I know how different in externals is Cézanne's work, but the impressiveness of this picture seems to go beyond that of the Gothic: it is to the even greater art of Greece that I say we must turn.

Mention has been made of those younger men who were asking reasons for the phenomena of art. Among these seekers for understanding, it is Seurat who goes furthest, for he not only puts questions but gives answers, and in writing. We have entered the age of consciousness, and if no final answers about art are ever to be given, a considerable step has been made when Seurat defines the functions of the vertical, the horizontal, and the oblique line, warm and cool color, etc. No longer could a piece of drawing be justified by its likeness to something in nature. What makes "good drawing" was always a matter of the third dimension, of form as a whole, as character, or of design and the other classic qualities. Long before one knows that Seurat had been the devoted student of a favorite pupil of Ingres's, one can see in him the qualities of the marvelous draftsman. They are in the paintings, above all perhaps in the earliest masterpiece, the *Boys Bathing* (see Plate 40), but also in the beautiful drawings in conté crayon. *The Clearing* (see Plate 39), although a painting, contains the qualities of the conté drawings and is invaluable in showing their decisive influence on his masterpieces. Sometimes the black-and-white studies come into sharp focus, as in the portrait of Signac, a thing as fine as a Pisanello medal; but usually they are rather blurred silhouettes through which the artist makes his powerful analysis of mass and tone. With such qualities well in hand, he could go on to effects of color, which he analyzed in repeated studies from nature.

The methodical thoroughness shown in thus dividing up the processes of picture-making earned for Seurat the epithet of pedant in some quarters. Something of the kind was at the root of Renoir's opposition to him. The accusation is ill based: pedantry presupposes a body of established rules or practice, whereas Seurat creates his procedure according to his own needs. In his art, Ingres's sense of form meets the sense of color for which Seurat's intensive study of Delacroix was the basis. Such a uniting of qualities which at first sight seem unreconcilable bespeaks an eclectic mind of the type which the Greeks had when they breathed the breath of life into their fusion of Oriental and Western values.

In the last and greatest of Seurat's pictures, *The Circus* (see Plate 41), how romantically free he is with all those delightful beings, the dainty equestrienne with her flying horse, the clowns, the ringmaster, the orchestra, and the carefully portrayed members of the public. Reliving our pleasure in such details we need to put them into their places in the marvelous overall design of the picture. Then we see the artist's unifying control of all the components of the great effect, its human elements as just recalled and the pointillism which, with its thousands of tiny touches, bathes the whole scene in its unbroken light. I need not point out how classical is the mind that thus orchestrates its resources. Here is perhaps our clearest example of the ancient fire in modern art.

To have said any such thing back in the nineties would have been to convict oneself of incompetence or insincerity with all but a handful of people, mostly artists. But appreciation has moved on at a brisker

pace since then, and Matisse's *Mme. Matisse,* 1913 (see Plate 42), **was**
recognized for the masterpiece that it is in a very brief time. **But still**
there would be some member of the rear guard to grumble, "A masterpiece, do you say? It's nothing but a mask." Very good; all there was
of Greek comedy and tragedy was spoken through masks. It is no small
thing to have made us feel again the expressiveness of such a simplifica-
tion (which, incidentally, still retains much of Mme. Matisse's features). "Every detail which is not essential," as the painter used to say,
"is occupying the space which ought to have been reserved for a detail
that is necessary there." At this late day it would seem that no one can
remain indifferent to the felicity, exemplified by the design of the hat,
let us say, with which the painter carried out the logic of his design.

After following him through the unemotional aloofness of his
purely classical study (and he spent more than a hundred sittings on
this portrait), we realize the wealth of his resources when we reach his
lithograph of the *Odalisque with Magnolias* (see Plate 43). Here the
voluptuous feminine figure, the luxurious design of the leaves, and the
unmistakable suggestion of color tell of a warmer climate in Matisse's
art. He knew his own character: to have continued too long in the
Spartan mood of the great *Mme. Matisse* would have been risking im-
poverishment, to have gone on too long with the glamour of the
Odalisque would have belied his need for new research—always an
intimate demand of Matisse's nature. By turning alternately from one
to the other type of work, Matisse retained the suppleness and health
which remained with him to the end.

A parallel choice of qualities is met when we consider our two
examples of Picasso's phenomenal art (see Plates 44 and 45). I emphasize my opinion that he is really a phenomenon. From his teens,
the abnormally early age when he began to paint important pictures,
until today, he has kept up an unbroken production of great extent
and, of course, of almost incredible inventiveness. Once he said to a
friend of mine, "I am like one of those whipping tops: as long as I
feel that lash of new sensation, I spin; if ever I stopped having new
inspiration, I should slow down in my movement and should fall to
the ground." With all his admiration for Matisse, he is very different
from that quiet, persistent Northerner. I much prefer such a description of Matisse to the words "German professor" employed for him
before 1914, doubtless because of his brown beard and his thick-lensed

glasses. His immense sensibility is anything but German, and his capacity for radical change (in externals, at least) is at the poles from a professor's necessary reliance on accumulated facts.

With Picasso an almost diabolical ability to find new solutions to his problems makes us question, at times, whether it is not his inexhaustible skill that we admire. Fortunately, he has a strain in him of pure beauty and can successfully stand the test of his work contained in the simple but important question: "Do you love it; would you care to live with it?" From the many Picassos that rise above the level of mere innovation and that convince us of their beauty, I have selected the two reproduced in Plates 44 and 45. As remarked before, some people find it natural to like the lovely nymph of the lithograph and to find the cubistic canvas pretty hard swallowing. We need feel no concern if we get spontaneous admiration for the naturalistic figure: people are not falling for the pretty girl, even if their talk would permit so poor an estimate of their power of appreciation. Of course there is really present the romantic element of illustration (Leo Stein's word for the pre-cubistic Picassos). But nowhere in his Blue Period or his Rose Period is there this extravagant sensibility as to line: it could have come about only through his decisive contact with geometrical research.

And the classical discipline afforded him by a mathematical viewing of art was a guaranty against the illustrator's danger of sentimentality before a beautiful subject. John Sloan used to warn against over-attractiveness in one's models. "It's you," he would say, "who have to make them beautiful; otherwise you're just copying." Clear enough is the fact that cubism is the very reverse of "just copying." Not only is there no possibility in it for reproduction of the appearances of nature, but Ruskin's "create or perish" takes on a new significance in the presence of cubism. We see very well what has been sacrificed, and we demand an equal value in what has been added. Evidently the severe logic of geometrical construction is one gain— something that we can check on and—to an extent—pronounce successful or the reverse.

If we cannot be dead sure as to such a judgment, the reason lies in a deeper, more important virtue of the new concept. The renunciation of optical fidelity leaves the mind free to cast its own illumination on the subject. As the beam of a searchlight plays over a nocturnal scene, the Cubist lights up his model with a moving ray from which he derives now this angle or group of forms, now another one, giving them the amount of intensity that he prefers. One might almost say "disinterested" for the way he builds up his composition, meaning thereby that the subject has been deprived of the predominant importance it had before, and that the classical values of form and the rest have taken its place. That is the case with the *Female Nude* (see Plate 44). The sensuous appeal suggested by the title has been replaced by a sort of free logic leading to a hitherto undiscovered form. One would call it crystaline if that word did not suggest the work of merely chemical or physical forces. But this is clearly the product of a mind, and the rich variety of the tones—from deep black to shining white—could not have come about by such a process as gives us even the diamond. Picasso's long evolution from personal feeling for the poor circus people of his youth to the generalized tragedy of the *Guernica,* could not have reached the impressiveness of that latter work without such achievement as we see in *Female Nude.*

Is it ingratitude toward the man who has done so much for better understanding by all of us, if we breathe easier when we reach the work of Duchamp-Villon? Before a sculpture like his *Torso of a Young Man* (see Plate 46), we think for a moment to see no more of a departure from "nature" than is rendered by the robustly accentuated planes, and for these there is an ample supply of parallels in the work of many contemporaries who were trying to rescue themselves from the beguiling sensitiveness of Rodin's modeling. The nobility of proportions in this *Torso* is one thing to make us look further into its qualities; the almost impersonal treatment of the head is another such reason. The features are those of his brother, Marcel Duchamp, who posed for the sculptor, but the fact will come as a surprise to many who looked on the head as merely that of a type, a somewhat Greek type.

It became so through the same process of thought that gave to the body as a whole so much the quality of the *Warrior* of Aegina (see Plate 47). I have the strongest doubt that Duchamp-Villon was influenced by such casts of the Aegina figures as may be in Paris. I do not know that there are such, and certainly the French sculptor never saw the originals, which are in Munich. So we have again the case of Barye's painting and the *Girl with Cap* (see Plate 18). More closely, the relationship is that of the Géricault drawing and the *Ilyssus,* for in the latter case as in that of the Duchamp-Villon there is a margin of possibility that the modern artists knew the ancient works in reproduction, if not directly. There is also less of the wonder of the Barye case for the resemblance between the pairs of works is not complete, though striking enough. What is essential is the likeness, almost the identity, in the spirit of the modern works as compared with the ancient ones. The *Girl with Cap* has the perfection of the time just after Phidias; the Aegina figure is before the culminating time of the Greeks, it still smacks of the archaic. And this increases its likeness to the Duchamp-Villon *Torso,* a work done at a time of new beginnings.

There is a reason why the parallelism should not be complete. Barye, appearing at the time of the Greek Revival headed by Louis David, made his first studies under Baron Gros, the great representative of David as a teacher. It was natural, then, that his early and indeed later ideal should be neo-classical when he carried it out as perfectly as he did in the *Nude* of this book. But Duchamp-Villon came at a very different period. Instead of the calm surety of the men who based themselves on the classics, there was excitement in his time, when more and more new sources of inspiration were being tapped. We come to his Baudelaire (see Plate 48) which, on the testimony of a man who knew the great poet (as Duchamp-Villon never did—save, of course, through his writings) , is the best likeness of the man—himself an innovator. The sculptor's startling success in portraying his magnificent subject was due to his having impregnated his mind with Baudelaire's thought. It is not necessary to specify which period glows from the strong features before us. The time is evidently one for firm, constructive thinking—as was the Gothic time. The early thirteenth century and the early twentieth century faced big problems; Duchamp-Villon faced them as manfully as did the sculptor who produced the glorious *Head* on the Portail Royal at Chartres (see Plate 49) . If a medieval patience with detail as compared with the summary treatment of the modern time makes a difference between the two works, I maintain that the difference is one of surfaces, and does not get below them.

What counts is that the two Christian sculptors have given us symbols of thought. Thus, in the field where the romantic tendency is most strongly manifested, we see that Duchamp-Villon is as worthy of the past as he is in the confrontation with classical art represented by the *Torso* (as related to the Aegina figure). In the mere yesterday of forty years ago (the sculptor died in 1918, when still a young man), work could be done that bears comparison with masterpieces; the fact is of great importance. It means that modern art really does have the resources to go on from the dead end it faces in the so-called abstract school as well as in the academic art of today.

A reason for this optimism is the timelessness of much of the best work of our period. Derain, in his *Fauve* years may be said to date, however fine was his production a half century ago. But a work like the *Head* (see Plate 50) stands with things unaffected by the passing of time, like the portraits of the Fayum, the last great painting of Egypt. Yet its originality is typically of the present century, even while its profound character-rendering tempted me to mention it with the masters who gave us the Pompeiian *Baker and His Wife,* or that profound *Self Portrait* by Gros, or Rembrandt's luminous canvases. Matters of style offer us differences among these works, from pre-Christian days to those of Derain in our own century; but the essential matter of man's idea of his character and destiny remains unchanged.

We are prepared for a sense of stability when dealing with the classical qualities. Rightness of scale or of proportion is probably a matter of our physical make-up, just as the harmony or discord of two musical notes is based on elements in our physiology; and we get but little further than such a statement when we say arbitrarily that a detail in one art or another is right or wrong. But when we come to the romantic element in art, especially that of portraiture, we are apt to be surprised at its permanence. The fact that portraits covering two thousand years confirm one another as these do justifies that word "timelessness" which I used before when introducing the Derain.

It is not the first time that I tell of my final interview with Matisse, but a thing he said then seems to me so deeply important that I am glad of another opportunity to widen the circle of those who have heard it. Confined to the bed from which he was not to rise again, his eighty years and more of honesty led him to say, "The further I go, the more I am convinced that there is a right and wrong in conduct and likewise in art." Matisse had witnessed the conflict of ideas among the various art movements of his time, and had come to the conclusion that they were not questions of personal taste but that they rested on fundamental, permanent truths.

I am happy to have such confirmation of my own conception of art. Its symbol is the Phoenix, that bird in which the Greeks and other ancient peoples saw the continuance of true ideas. Their form would burn to ashes, from time to time, but always there was something indestructible which arose again, spreading its wings with new life. "Art is joyful!" exclaims Schiller in his poem saluting the inauguration of a new theater. If my illustrations reinforce this feeling as one follows the progression of the images, I shall have done well to offer their testimony to the public at a time which can use their renewed cause for confidence. The old fire of the classics burns afresh in our creative, romantic period.

1. **GREEK,** fifth century B.C.: **The Ilyssus from the Parthenon** (*British Museum*)

2. GÉRICAULT: Leda (*The Louvre*)

3. JEAN GOUJON: The Rivers of France (*Fontaine des Innocents, Paris*)

4. POUSSIN: The Realm of Flora (*Dresden*)

5. WATTEAU: The Judgment of Paris (*The Louvre*)

6. Louis David: The Sabines—detail (*The Louvre*)

7. DELACROIX: Fresco at Valmont (*Courtesy M. Beraldi, Valmont*)

8. DELACROIX: Autumn (*Museum of São Paulo, Brazil*)

9. DELACROIX: The Sibyl with the Golden Bough (*Private Collection, France*)

10. POMPEIIAN ART, first century B.C.: Woman with a Shield (*Metropolitan Museum of Art*)

11. Pompeiian Art, first century B.C.: Man and Woman (*Metropolitan Museum of Art*)

12. DELACROIX: Heliodorus (*Church of St. Sulpice, Paris*)

13. RAPHAEL: Heliodorus (Vatican)

14. **Pompeiian Art**: Centauress and Bacchante (*Museo Nazionale, Naples*)

15. **Delacroix**: Centauress and Bacchante (*Collection Walter Pach*)

16. DELACROIX: Achilles and the Centaur (*Private Collection, Paris*)

17. BARYE: Nude (*Collection Walter Pach*)

18. GREEK, about 400 B.C.: Girl with Cap (*Museum Antiker Kleinkunst, Munich*)

19. BARYE: Lapith (Theseus) and Centaur (*Metropolitan Museum of Art*)

20. BARYE: Three Graces (*Metropolitan Museum of Art*)

21. **Barye**: Jaguar and Hare (*The Louvre*)

22. BARYE: Leopard Resting (*Metropolitan Museum of Art*)

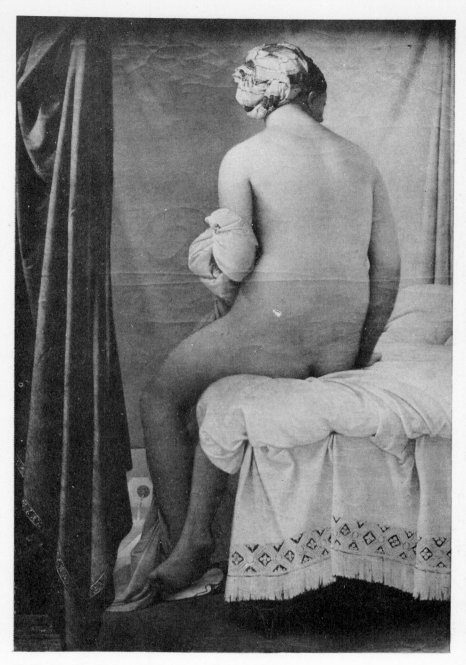

23. INGRES: The Bather of Valpinçon (*The Louvre*)

24. INGRES: Mme. Ingres (*Reinhardt Collection, Paris*)

25. COROT: Hagar and Ishmael (*Metropolitan Museum of Art*)

26. COROT: Woman with a Pearl (*The Louvre*)

27. LEONARDO DA VINCI: Mona Lisa (*The Louvre*)

28. BARON GROS: Self Portrait (*Versailles*)

29. Pompeiian Art: The Baker and His Wife (*Museo Nazionale, Naples*)

30. COURBET: Woman with a Parrot (*Metropolitan Museum of Art*)

31. MANET: Bar at the Folies Bergères (*Tate Gallery, London*)

32. RENOIR: Mother and Child (*Formerly collection Leo Stein*)

33. RENOIR: Girls Bathing (*Philadelphia Museum of Art*)

34. RENOIR: Two Women with Flowered Hats (*Courtesy Paul Rosenberg and Company*)

35. CÉZANNE: The Clockmaker (*The Solomon R. Guggenheim Museum*)

36. **CÉZANNE:** Landscape (*Fine Arts Museum, Basel*)

37. CÉZANNE: Still Life (*Municipal Art Gallery, Johannesburg*)

38. CÉZANNE: Water Color (*The Art Institute, Chicago*)

39. SEURAT: The Clearing (*Courtesy M. Knoedler and Company*)

40. Seurat: Boys Bathing (*Tate Gallery, London*)

41. SEURAT: The Circus (*The Louvre*)

42. MATISSE: Mme. Matisse (*Moscow*)

43. MATISSE: Odalisque with Magnolias

44. PICASSO: Female Nude (*Philadelphia Museum of Art*)

45. PICASSO: Nymph

46. DUCHAMP-VILLON: **Torso of a Young Man** (*Collection Alexander M. Bing*)

47. GREEK, fifth century B.C.: Warrior of Aegina *(Glyptothek, Munich)*

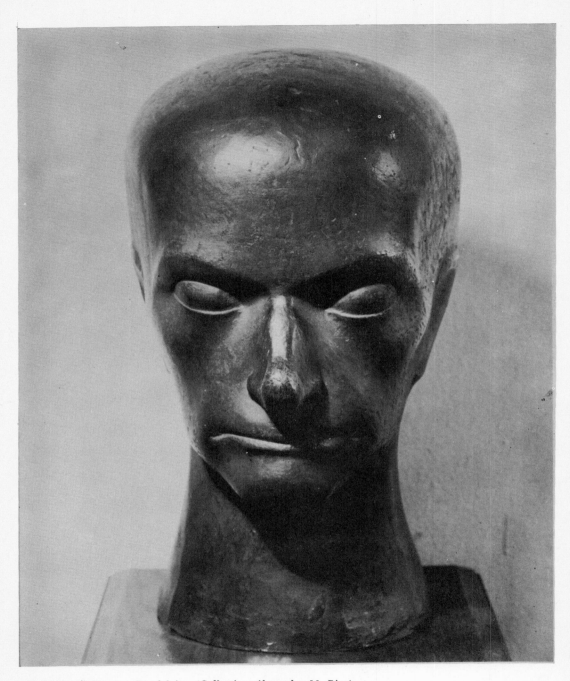

48. **Duchamp-Villon:** Baudelaire *(Collection Alexander M. Bing)*

49. FRENCH, thirteenth century: Head (*Chartres Cathedral*)

50. DERAIN: Head (*Private Collection*)